T0058929

# THE ACOUSTIC GUITAR METHOD
## CHORD BOOK

### by DAVID HAMBURGER

This edition can be used on its own, or as a supplement to *The Acoustic Guitar Method*

**Editor:** Jeffrey Pepper Rodgers

**Cover photograph:** Rory Earnshaw

**Author photograph:** Todd Wolfson

ISBN 978-0-634-05082-4

STRING LETTER PUBLISHING

EXCLUSIVELY DISTRIBUTED BY

HAL•LEONARD® CORPORATION

7777 W. BLUEMOUND RD. P.O. BOX 13819 MILWAUKEE, WI 53213

Visit Hal Leonard Online at
**www.halleonard.com**

In Australia Contact:
Hal Leonard Australia Pty. Ltd.
22 Taunton Drive P.O. Box 5130
Cheltenham East, 3192 Victoria, Australia
Email: ausadmin@halleonard.com

# CHORD NOTATION KEY

Chord diagrams show where the fingers go on the fingerboard. Frets are shown horizontally, and the thick top line represents the nut. The sixth (lowest-pitched) string is on the far left, and first (highest-pitched) string is on the far right. Dots show where the fingers go, and the numbers above the diagram tell you which fretting-hand fingers to use: 1 for the index finger, 2 the middle, 3 the ring, 4 the pinky, and *T* the thumb. An *X* indicates a string that should be muted or not played; 0 indicates an open string.

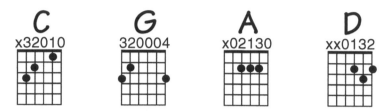

A solid line across two or more strings indicates a barre, or the use of one finger to cover more than one string at a time.

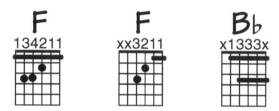

Chords that include notes above the fifth fret are shown without the thick line representing the nut; the Roman numeral to the right indicates which fret to play the chord at. The Roman numeral always refers to the lowest fret used in the chord, which is not always being played on the lowest string in the chord.

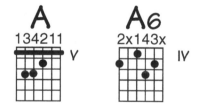

When a chord includes notes above the fifth fret and has one or more open strings as well, it is shown without the thick line representing the nut, a Roman numeral to the right indicating the lowest fretted note in the chord, and 0's for any open strings.

# CONTENTS

# INTRODUCTION

This book presents chords by key in all 12 keys, offering both open-position (using open strings) and closed-position (no open strings) voicings where possible for each common type of chord. In folk, bluegrass, blues, and other roots-music styles, guitarists favor basic chords in keys that allow them to use lots of open strings (namely the keys of A, C, D, E, and G). But it's a big universe of chords out there, and this book can help you navigate through it and discover some new options. Don't be intimidated by all the sharps and flats and fancy chord names; use the portions of this book that apply to what you're playing right now, and then you can come back to the rest as your chord vocabulary expands.

For a better understanding of where all these shapes are coming from, you may want to take a spin through the opening sections first. Chords come in families, and there is a logic to both how they are fingered and what they are called. We'll start with a discussion of what chords actually are and how they are named, and proceed to lessons on barre chords (with some hints on how to get better at playing them) and other closed-position fingerings. Then comes the Chord Library, arranged alphabetically by key. Finally, we close by talking about how to get the most out of the open-position sound on the guitar (and make your life easier) via judicious use of the capo and learning a little bit about transposing a song from one key to another.

As you encounter unfamiliar chords in a songbook or other source, use this book as a resource to locate the simplest and/or most appropriate voicing for the chord that's called for. As you do so, you will naturally expand your chord vocabulary in one of the best ways possible, because playing songs with new chords in them is a great way to get new chord shapes under your fingers for good.

*Need help with this book? Ask a question in our free, online support forum in the Guitar Talk section of www.acousticguitar.com.*

# WHAT CHORD NAMES MEAN

How many times have you flipped open a songbook or a chord chart and been baffled by something peculiar like A7♭13♯9? Or been put off by something just out of the ordinary like Dm6? It may seem like these names were designed to deliberately confuse you, but in fact they're trying to tell you very specific things about what to play. In this section we'll look at how chords get their names and break down what some of those more obscure-sounding names really mean.

## MAJOR AND MINOR TRIADS

First things first: the most basic kind of chord is called a *triad*, because it boils down to just three notes. If you look at an open A-major chord and name the notes in it from bottom to top, it's got A, E, A, C♯, and A. Tossing out the duplicate A and E notes, you're left with A, C♯, and E. These three notes are the essence of the chord, which you can hear by just strumming the top three strings of an open A chord. Likewise, if you looked at, say, a G-major chord going from the lowest to the highest strings, you'd find the notes G, B, D, G, B, and G. But when you throw out all the duplicate notes, it just amounts to G, B, and D, which you can hear if you play just the bottom three notes of the chord.

A
x02130

Notes: A E A C♯ E

G
320004

Notes: G B D G B G

You can determine the notes in the chord by relating them to a scale with the same root as the chord. For example, here are the notes of an A-major scale.

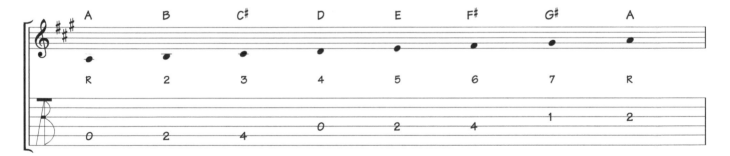

Just by counting, you can see that A is the first note (or *root*) of the scale, C♯ is the third note, and E is the fifth note. And that's how they're referred to when they're the notes of an A major chord: A is called the root, C♯ is called the third, and E is called the fifth.

It's the C♯, or third of the chord, that makes an A major sound like A major. When you simply see the chord symbol A it means *A major*, which in turn means a chord that includes at least one A, one C♯, and one E. There can be more than one of any of those notes, but no other notes (no F's or G♭'s, for instance). And the notes can be *voiced* in any order: that is, the A doesn't have to be on the bottom, nor does the C♯ have to be in the middle or the E on top. In our original A-chord example, the lowest note is an A but the next note up is the fifth, E, followed by another A, and then the third and the fifth again on the top two strings.

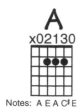

Notes: A E A C♯ E            A E A C E

You can also have a *minor triad*. The only difference between a major triad and a minor triad is its third. You can see and hear this by playing an A-major chord and then switching to an A-minor chord.

The only note to change is the third: C♯ gets lowered a half step, to C♮. In a major chord, the third is what we call a *major third:* that note is the interval of a major third (two steps, or four frets) above the root. As you might guess, a minor chord has a *minor third:* a step and a half, or three frets, up from the root. If we look at all five notes of an open A minor, we've got: A, E, A, C, E. Once we toss all the duplicate notes, we're left with A, C, E, or root, minor third, fifth. So when you see the chord name Am, it means any combination or collection of notes that has at least one and possibly more than one A, C, and E, in any order, and no other notes.

So now we know why major and minor chords are called major and minor. As we've just seen, an A chord can be either one. When you see a chord name, the first part, the letter, is the root, while whatever follows refers to the *quality*. In the case of an A-major chord, the root is A, and the quality is major. With an A-minor chord, the root is still A, but the quality is minor.

## AUGMENTED AND DIMINISHED TRIADS

Now we know what happens when the third is major or minor; what happens to a triad if the fifth changes?

The fifth found in both the major and minor triad is called a *perfect fifth.* There are three and a half steps (seven frets) between the root and a perfect fifth. If you take an A-major triad and raise the fifth a half step to E♯, you have the interval (A to E♯) of an *augmented fifth,* and the resulting chord, A C♯ E♯, is called A *augmented.* Raise the high string one fret in our three-note A chord to hear what it sounds like.

Going in the opposite direction, if you take an A-minor triad and lower the fifth by a half step, you've got the interval (A to E♭) of a *diminished fifth,* and the resulting chord, A–C–E♭, is called an A diminished. It takes a little tricky fingering up the neck to hear what a three-note *A diminished* chord sounds like.

So we've got four kinds of triads: major, minor, augmented, and diminished. Here they are, in terms of their roots, thirds, and fifths.

| 5 | 5 | +5 | ♭5 |
|---|---|---|---|
| 3 | ♭3 | 3 | ♭3 |
| R | R | R | R |
| *major* | *minor* | *augmented* | *diminished* |

## SEVENTHS

In a scale or a chord, a seventh is the seventh note up from the root. Looking at our A-major scale, the seventh is G♯. From A to G♯ is in fact a *major seventh,* or an interval of five and a half steps. A *minor seventh* is one half step smaller than a major seventh, or an interval of five whole steps. For example, a minor seventh up from A is G♮.

As a shortcut when dealing with chords, you might try thinking of the major seventh as just a half step below the root, and the minor seventh as a whole step below the root. (If that just leaves you more confused, forget I ever said anything about it.)

The various kinds of seventh chords you may have seen or heard about are just triads with an interval of a seventh up from the root added on. The question is, what kind of seventh—major or minor—is being added on to what kind of triad: major, minor, augmented, or diminished?

To keep things relatively simple, let's leave the augmented and diminished triads out of it for now, and stick to just major and minor triads and sevenths. You've basically got four possibilities: major triad with major seventh, major triad with minor seventh, minor triad with major seventh, minor triad with major seventh. Whoo! Is your head spinning yet? Try thinking of it in a little grid like the one at right.

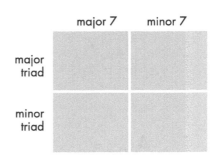

There's a different name for the result of each one of these combinations. Two of them are pretty logical. If you add a major seventh to a major triad, the result is called a *major seventh* chord. Similarly, if you add a minor seventh to a minor triad, the result is called a *minor seventh* chord. These are usually abbreviated maj7 and min7 (or m7). So when you see Amaj7, you can think to yourself, "Aha! Everything major—an A major triad with a major seventh on top." Since the seventh note of an A-major scale is G♯, what you need is an A-major chord with a G♯ buried in the middle or perched on top. In other words, one of the two examples at right.

Likewise, when you see Am7, you can unpack it by thinking, "Yes, yes, I see, everything minor . . . an A-minor triad with a G♮ added in," since G♮ is a half step lower than the major seventh, G♯, and therefore is the minor seventh of A. Either one of the chords shown would fit the bill nicely, with a G♮ either insinuated into the midst of the chord or waving around conspicuously on the high end.

So far, so good. But now, alas, is where things get a little peculiar. What do you call a major triad with a minor seventh on top? Not a major seventh chord, because the seventh itself is minor. And not a minor seventh chord, because the triad itself is major. This hybrid of major and minor is called a *dominant seventh* chord. Confusion can ensue quickly, because a dominant seventh chord is generally referred to as simply a *seventh chord:* an A dominant seventh chord, for example, is simply written A7, not Adom7. So you need to know a couple of things: when you see A7, it means A dominant seventh, and that in turn means an A-major triad with a minor seventh added, or an A-major chord plus a G♮, which would look like one of the two chords at right.

The last possibility, a minor triad with a major seventh, is pretty rare, so we won't worry about it too much. It's also notated the most literally: an A-minor triad with a G♯ or major seventh added is written Am(maj7). Imagine that.

Going back to our diagram, then, we can fill it in as shown.

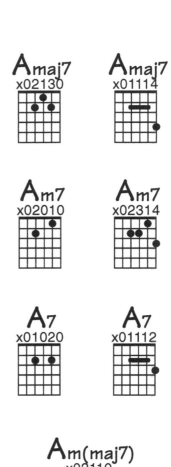

|  | major 7 | minor 7 |
|---|---|---|
| major triad | maj7 chord | dom7 chord |
| minor triad | m(maj)7 chord | m7 chord |

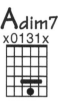

Now, what about adding sevenths to augmented and diminished triads? When an augmented triad has a seventh added to it, it's usually a minor seventh. Since the result is basically a dominant seventh chord (because of the major third in the triad and the minor seventh on top) with an augmented fifth, the chord is called an *augmented seventh* chord. Check out this Aaug7.

A diminished triad usually has only a minor seventh added to it. You'd think the resulting chord would have the decency to be called a diminished seventh chord, but it does not. It is called, instead, a *minor seven flat five chord*, which is really just about the chord name to end all chord names. And yet, if you peel it apart, it does make sense. The minor third of the diminished triad and the minor seventh on top basically add up to a minor seventh chord. But there's the diminished fifth of the diminished triad. And a diminished fifth is a perfect fifth made a half step smaller, or flatted. So, a minor seven flat five chord is just trying to tell you: "I'm a minor triad with a minor seventh added. Oh, and by the way, my fifth has been flatted as well." This takes up too much room on the page, so it's written m7♭5. Now you know what that means. Here's an Am7♭5 to try.

There *is* such a thing as a diminished seventh chord. It's a diminished triad with a diminished seventh interval added to it (a diminished seventh is a minor seventh that's been made one half step smaller). So it makes a certain kind of sense: a maj7 chord is a major triad plus a major seventh interval, a m7 chord is a minor triad plus a minor seventh interval, and a dim7 chord is a diminished triad plus a diminished seventh. Try out the Adim7 to the left.

## SIXTHS

Sixths are, relatively speaking, a piece of cake. You only really need to worry about adding major sixths to triads, and only to the major and minor triads. A major sixth is a whole step above the fifth, or four and a half steps up from the root. In the key of A, for example, the major sixth is F♯.

A major triad with a major sixth added is called a *major sixth* chord. A minor triad with a major sixth added is called a *minor sixth* chord. You might see the major version notated as either A6 or Amaj6; the minor version is always fully notated, for example, Am6. Try out one of each.

## FIVE CHORDS

Theory ideally follows practice, and in recent years guitar chord notation has caught up with what actually goes on in the real world, namely, that plenty of times guitarists abbreviate their chords by just pounding out the bottom two strings of the chord, or the root and fifth. True rockers know this is called a *power chord*; those of us responsible for notating the results put such chords in print as *five chords*, as in C5, A5, E♭5, etc. That just means all there is to the chord is the root and the fifth. Actually, you can have more than two strings involved so long as the only notes included are duplicates of the root and fifth. Try out the two-string versions of A5 and D5, and then mute the fifth string for the big strummy G5.

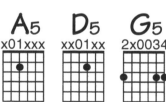

## SUS4, SUS2, ADD2

Asus4
x01240

*Sus* stands for *suspended*. The idea is that having the fourth of the chord temporarily replace the third creates a feeling of suspense, of waiting for the fourth to resolve back to the third. The fourth degree of the scale is just a half step above the third, so to create a sus4 chord, you raise the third of a major triad up one fret. To play an Asus4 chord, change the C♯ on the second string (second fret) to a D (third fret). Aren't you just dying to bring it back to the second fret? OK, you're dying to play the rest of "Pinball Wizard." Understood.

Asus2
x02300

*Sus2* is a more modern idea along the same lines: you replace the third with the *second* step of the scale. Guitarists like this because, like five chords, sus2 chords create a certain ambiguity, being neither major nor minor. They don't really have the same strong pull to resolve that sus4 chords do, so the sus part of sus2 is bit of a misnomer. On an A chord, the second is B. Let the second string ring open on an open A chord and you've got the sound of Asus2.

*Add 2* means just what it says: add the second interval to the chord. So, Am add2 means take an A-minor triad and add the second, while Aadd2 means take an A-major triad and add the second. The subtle distinction between sus2 and add2 is that you add the second to an add2 chord, so the third—major or minor—is still present. That takes a little fancy fingerwork sometimes, but the results are cool.

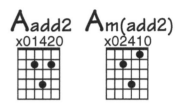

Aadd2
x01420

Am(add2)
x02410

## NINTHS, 11THS, AND 13THS

You knew it would come to this, didn't you?

Well, look, it's not as bad as it seems. To begin with, ninths, 11ths, and 13ths are just slick names for seconds, fourths, and sixths played an octave up. Check it out: if you took a major scale (what the heck, let's use an A-major scale) and wrote it out in two octaves, you'd get what's shown below:

Now, let's number all the notes. When we get to the octave, we'll just keep going:

So B, which is the second, is also the ninth; D, which is the fourth, is also the 11th; and F♯, the sixth, is also the 13th.

"So," I hear you wondering, "just when is it a sixth and when is it a 13th? For that matter, when is it a second and when is it a ninth?" Well, the answer is actually pretty straightforward. Anytime you add a second, fourth, or sixth to just a triad, as we did earlier, it's called a second, fourth, or sixth. Anytime you add a

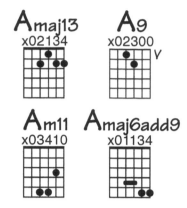

second, fourth, or sixth to some kind of *seventh* chord, it's called by its upper name: that is, ninth, 11th, or 13th. When added to a chord, ninths, 11ths, and 13ths are usually called *upper extensions*.

That way, if you see the notation A6, you know that it's just an A-major triad with a sixth added. If, however, you see Amaj13, it means an Amaj7 chord with a sixth added.

Major seventh and dominant seventh chords are more likely to have ninths and 13ths added. Minor seventh chords are more likely to have ninths and 11ths added. You may occasionally run into something called a 6add9 chord, which, just as its name suggests, is a major sixth chord with a ninth added. The point is, it has a sixth rather than the seventh included in a major ninth chord.

## ALTERED EXTENSIONS: ♭9, ♯9, ♯11 AND ♭13

It may seem like we're really getting into the stratosphere, but again, once you know what the symbols all mean, it's really not that out there.

An altered extension is basically a ninth, 11th, or 13th that has been raised (sharped) or lowered (flatted) a half step. It's considered "altered" because once raised or lowered, it is no longer *diatonic*, or what you would naturally get by just climbing up the scale to get to the interval of that number.

Ironically, altered extensions pretty much live a tame life, as they tend to attach themselves only to dominant seventh chords (with one exception we'll get to in a second). The four possibilities are: ♭9, ♯9, ♯11, and ♭13. There's no point in flatting the 11, since the result would be another third in the chord. And raising the 13th would likewise result in adding another ♭7 to the chord. So on an A7 chord, where 9, 11, and 13 are B, D, and F♯, the possible altered extensions are B♭ (♭9), C (♯9), D♯ (♯11), and F♮ (♭13). As a rule, we add either ♭9 or ♯9, with or without the ♭13 as well, or just the ♯11. The ♯11 is also the one altered extension that can be applied to the major seventh chord.

One further note: altered extensions, unlike ordinary or "natural" ninths, 11ths, and 13ths, are written out following the name of the seventh chord they've been added to. So, for example, while an Amaj7 chord with a natural ninth added is written Amaj9, an Amaj7 chord with a ♯11 added is notated Amaj7♯11. Likewise, while A13 indicates an A dominant 13 chord with a natural 13 added, when an altered 13th is added, it's notated A7♭13.

So now, when you see something inscrutable like A7♭13♯9, just take a deep breath and pull it apart: it's an A dominant seventh chord—that's an A major triad with a minor seventh on top—with a ♭13 added (a 13th is the same as a sixth, and in this case it's flatted, or lowered a half step) and a ♯9 as well (a ninth being the same as a second, and in this case raised a half step).

It can be done! The chord symbols are just trying to tell you what's there. Over time, you'll learn and remember a handful of open and movable chord shapes that your fingers will jump to when they see these various symbols, and your life will become one long groovy chord parade.

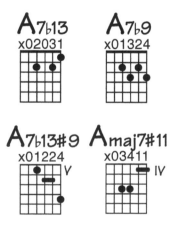

# BARRE CHORDS

Playing a *barre chord* involves holding down most or all of the strings across a single fret (i.e., in a "barre" across the fingerboard) and using some combination of your remaining three fretting fingers to form the rest of the chord. Since they have no open strings, barre chords sound really different from open chords and are part of the family of movable chord shapes. Any chord with no open strings is considered a movable chord shape. A movable chord shape can be played anywhere on the neck, and it takes its name from whatever note its root is on at the time.

Barre chords have a reputation for being hard on your hand, so we'll look at how to practice and play barre chords as well as how to know when and where to use them.

## THE E AND A SHAPES

Barre chords come in two basic shapes. If you've played an open E chord or an open A chord, you should recognize where these new fingerings come from.

The first one is like a capoed E chord, only your index finger is acting as the capo. The second one is like a capoed A chord with your index finger acting like the capo. One difference with the A-shape chord is that you can't really get the high string to sound at the third fret unless your ring finger is double-jointed. At the same time, you don't want to hear the high string fretted at the fifth fret either, so try raising your ring finger at that point just enough to mute the high string, which most people's hands are flexible enough to allow. Alternatively, you can make the main barre with your index finger and then use your remaining fingers to individually fret the fourth, third, and second strings.

The cool thing about barre chords is that you can move one shape around to get all kinds of chords. "Aha," I hear you say, "and just how do I know what chord I'm playing if they all look the same?" Good point. The idea is that since this first shape is like capoing an E chord, and the root of an E chord is on the sixth string, any barre chord we play using this shape will take its name from whatever note our index finger is covering on the sixth string. That's why this chord shape is also called a *sixth-string-root* voicing. If you play this shape at the third fret, you get a G chord, because the root note of the chord (on the sixth string) is a G. Move up a whole step to the fifth fret and now your index finger is on A, so you've got an A chord. Here's a table of some of the main chords you can get moving the E-shape barre chord up the neck.

Let's check out the A shape (remember, it's like capoing an A chord with your index finger taking the place of the capo). This shape is sort of a double whammy, because in addition to barring with your index finger, you're also barring the rest of the required notes with your ring finger at the same time. But there is some good news: you're only covering five strings with your index finger instead of six, and the only one that really has to ring clear is the fifth string itself. Also, the high string is supposed to be muted by the underside of your ring finger, which is probably happening without your even trying. If the high

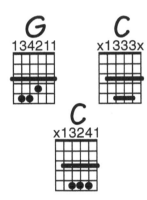

### E-Shape Barre Chords

| Fret | Chord |
| --- | --- |
| 1 | F |
| 3 | G |
| 5 | A |
| 7 | B |
| 8 | C |
| 10 | D |

## A-Shape Barre Chords

| Fret | Chord |
|------|-------|
| 1 | B♭ |
| 2 | B |
| 3 | C |
| 5 | D |
| 7 | E |
| 8 | F |
| 10 | G |

**G5**
13xxxx

**C5**
x13xxx

**E**
023100

**Em**
023000

**G**
134211

**Gm**
134111

**A**
x02130

**Am**
x02310

**C**
x1333x

**Cm**
x13421

string is ringing out, giving you that end-of-a-Beatles-song sound (a major sixth chord, just so you know), let up the pressure a little with your ring finger at the high string and you should be able to mute it. Finally, if you're not doing so already, put your thumb along the back of the neck for more leverage.

The A-shape barre chord has its root on the fifth string (which is why the shapes based on it are sometimes referred to as *fifth-string-root voicings*), so if you can name a few notes on the fifth string, you can find your way around. Here's a table of where you can find some of those most-wanted chords.

*Power chords* are just the bottom two notes of a barre chord—the root and fifth of the chord. Electric guitarists use them because all those extra tones on the upper strings clutter things up and clash with each other when you pour them through a loud, distorted amp. Plus, they're a lot easier to play, especially when your guitar is hanging somewhere around your knees. Check out these two movable 5 chord forms.

Let's move beyond the basic major-chord shapes to learn about minor and dominant seventh barre chords, and look at movable chords with partial barres, too.

## MINOR CHORDS

Go back to open position for a moment, and compare an open E chord and an open E-minor chord. The only difference is that note on the third string. By lowering the G♯ on the first fret to an open G♮, you turn E major into E minor.

Now, back to the barre chords. If the sixth-string-root barre chord is just an E-major chord moved up the neck, we'll be able to make a minor barre chord by changing just one note too. Check out the before and after diagrams for changing G major into G minor. In some ways the new chord is easier to play because you have one less finger to hold down. But your index finger now has to barre more strings. Getting that third string to sound clearly will probably take some time.

You can also adapt the fifth-string-root barre chord into a minor voicing, using the same logic. Note the difference between open A and open A minor: you're lowering the C♯ to a C♮. We can turn a C barre chord at the third fret into a C-minor barre chord by changing just one note: the E to an E♭ on the second string. Changing one note here is a little more complicated than just dropping one finger from the chord; you need to actually switch from a three-string barre with your ring finger to putting your index, middle, and ring fingers down on individual notes. But just looking at the shapes should help you remember what to do: you're lowering the major third of the chord to a minor third.

## SEVENTH CHORDS

How else can we milk these two basic shapes? Go back to the open position again. Starting with the basic E chord, you can form E7 by dropping out the fretted root note, leaving a ♭7 to ring out in the middle of the chord. (The ♭7 is D♮, now heard on the open D string.) Once again, we'll move this idea up the fretboard. To change a G barre chord into G7, remove your pinky from the chord form so that the G note on the third string becomes an F. You have to pay more attention to your index finger to get that fourth-string note to ring out. It may be getting muted by either your ring finger or your index finger. This is OK for now. Your fingers will get stronger, and the chords will gradually start to sound clearer.

You can also convert fifth-string-root barre chords into dominant seventh chords. First look at the difference between open A and open A7. To get the seventh of the chord, you need to drop the A on the G string down to an open G (the ♭7 of the chord). With a C barre chord, it's going to be the same kind of adjustment, only the fingering change is going to be a little more radical (see the fingerings for C and C7 barre chords at the third fret).

Notice the relationship between the fingering of the open A7 chord and the corresponding C7.

## MINOR SEVENTHS

We can also get minor seventh barre chord forms out of these two basic shapes. In the open position, you would change an E-minor chord into an Em7 the same way as we changed E major into E7—by letting the fourth string ring open with the sound of the ♭7. Now with a sixth-string-root G-minor barre chord at the third fret, add in the minor seventh by lifting off your pinky. You're now fretting everything but the fifth string with your index finger at the third fret.

Likewise, you can convert an open Am to Am7 the same way you would change an open A major to A7—by letting the third string, the ♭7 of A, ring out. Moving this idea up the neck, start with a fifth-string-root Cm at the third fret and lift off your pinky, so that you're now barring the fifth, third, and first strings all with your index finger at the third fret.

## MINOR SEVEN FLAT FIVE

One more useful and closely related chord form with a fifth-string root is the m7♭5 shape. Take the fifth-string-root minor seventh chord and lower the fourth-string note (the fifth of the chord), by a half step, or one fret. Mute the other fifth, on the high string, and fret each note with a separate finger. Alternatively, you can mute the fourth string and lower the high string a half step, again fingering each note individually.

# OTHER CLOSED-POSITION CHORDS

A *closed-position* chord is any chord involving no open strings. The barre-chord shapes we covered in the last lesson are one example. There are also chords with partial barres, or just three or four strings barred, and chords where you only play three or four strings altogether and avoid or mute the remaining strings. Some of these chords make slightly easier substitutes for barre chords when you're just starting out; others are the only way to create certain kinds of sounds on the guitar. In all cases, since these chord shapes don't use open strings, you can move them all over the neck, and they simply take on the name of whatever note the root of the chord is at the time.

## PARTIAL BARRES

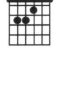

First, let's look at some abbreviated versions of the barre chords we've just learned. If you find the full five- and six-string barre chords too hard to get clear right now, you can try these shortened versions. They usually involve dropping out the lower strings, which often means you have no root on the bottom of the chord, or simply less bass to the chord overall. This also means that you may need to *avoid* strumming low strings that are no longer part of the chord. Despite these drawbacks, abbreviated barre chords provide you with a way to get certain sounds, like B♭, Bm, E♭, F, and F♯ chords, that simply don't exist in open position, without resorting to a full barre-chord voicing.

Let's start with a barre chord with a sixth-string root: F, at the first fret. You'll still need a small two-string barre at the first fret to play F major in its abbreviated form on just the top four strings. Alternatively, you may be able to catch the first and second strings together by putting your index finger down in between them in the normal, nonbarring way.

Now, by making various changes to this four-string major chord, we can create the movable 7th, 6th, minor, minor 7th, and minor 6th chords shown below:

Turning to the fifth-string-root barre shape, let's abbreviate a first-fret voicing of B♭. You can replace the ring-finger barre with your ring, middle, and pinky fingers each playing one note, and your index finger grabbing only the first fret on the high string. We can also alter this four-string major chord to create the 7th, minor and minor seventh chords shown below:

Changing the ring-finger barre to an index-finger barre at the third fret allows you to create four other voicings as well, for B♭, B♭maj7, B♭7, and B♭6.

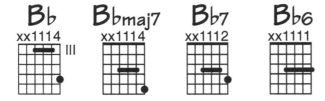

## REDUCING BARRE CHORDS

Another way to sidestep playing a full six-string barre is to finger only the most important notes of the chord. Reducing chord voicings to their essentials also creates a less cluttered and more transparent sound often favored by jazz and swing guitarists.

Let's pick up with a C7 barre chord from the E-shaped family at the eighth fret. Omitting and muting the fifth and first strings leaves us with this voicing, played with one finger per string.

Raising the note on the fourth string one fret and refingering accordingly gives us a Cmaj7 voicing; lowering it one fret instead creates a Cmaj6 chord.

Raising the second string of the C7 chord two frets creates a C13 chord; raising it just one fret creates a C7♭13 chord, also called Caug7.

The C7, Cmaj7, and Cmaj6 chords can all be played as just three-string chords as well, by muting the second string for an even sparer sound.

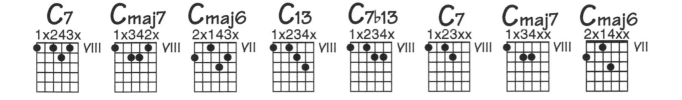

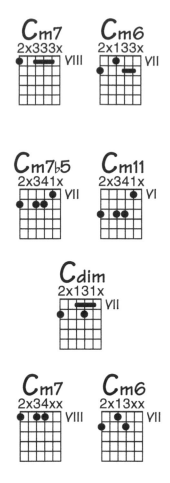

Doing this kind of surgery on the family of E-shaped minor chords still requires a *little* barring—this time with the ring finger. If we take a full Cm7 bar chord and leave out the fifth and first strings as we did with C7, we'll need to barre the fourth, third, and second strings with the ring finger. It's a lot like making the ring-finger barre on the A-shape family of barre chords. In this case, you could in fact barre all four top strings, but since we're going for a less cluttered sound as well as an easier fingering, let the top string go muted if you can.

Dropping the fourth string one fret changes the chord to a minor sixth voicing; now your barre really only covers the third and second strings.

Starting again from the minor seventh voicing and dropping the second string one fret creates a m7♭5 voicing, for which you've got to finger each string individually. Dropping the second string yet another fret yields a m11 chord form.

Let's take the m7♭5 chord a step further. Forming an abbreviated barre one fret down from your second finger, covering the fourth, third, and second strings, and continuing to finger the sixth and third strings at the eighth fret creates a full diminished, or diminished seventh, chord voicing.

The Cm7 and Cm6 chord voicings can both be further abbreviated by muting the second string and fretting the remaining three strings individually.

This approach lends itself well to several fifth-string-root minor chords as well. By starting with a minor seventh chord, leaving out the fourth string, and refingering the chord, we get a lighter, less clunky voicing on the fifth, third, second, and first strings.

Lowering the third string a half step gives us a minor sixth chord, while lowering the first string instead gives us a m7♭5 voicing.

The minor seventh and minor sixth chords can both be further abbreviated as three-string voicings.

  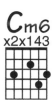

## THE C SHAPE

The last family of closed-position chords we'll look at is based around a third open chord shape: the C-chord shape. First, notice that with a basic C7 chord in open position, the middle four strings are all fretted, which means you can move it up the neck as long as you avoid or mute the high and low strings.

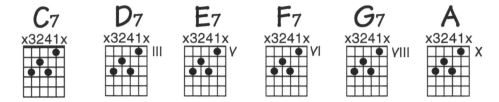

Let's look at some of the possibilities this shape offers, using F7 as our starting point.

Raise the note on the second string two frets and you've got F9, using all your fingers. By making a three-string barre with your ring finger, you can form another F9 that includes the high string as well. If you raise your pinkie one fret instead of forming the ring-finger barre, it creates F7#9, or "the 'Purple Haze' chord." Form a barre with your index finger at the seventh fret to create F7b9.

If you take the first F9 we played and lower your index finger one fret, it creates Fm9. Mute the fourth string and grab the high string at the sixth fret to form F11 (also called Eb/F).

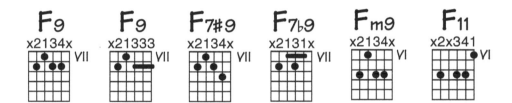

You can also form a few major seventh and major sixth voicings from this general shape; try the Fmaj7 and Fmaj6 below. In jazz and western swing, the maj6 form is often played with the fifth of the chord in the bass.

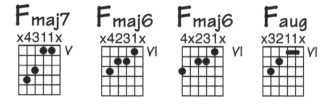

Finally, there's a movable augmented chord that comes out of this same family of chords. It involves a two-string barre at the sixth fret.

# CHORD LIBRARY
## A

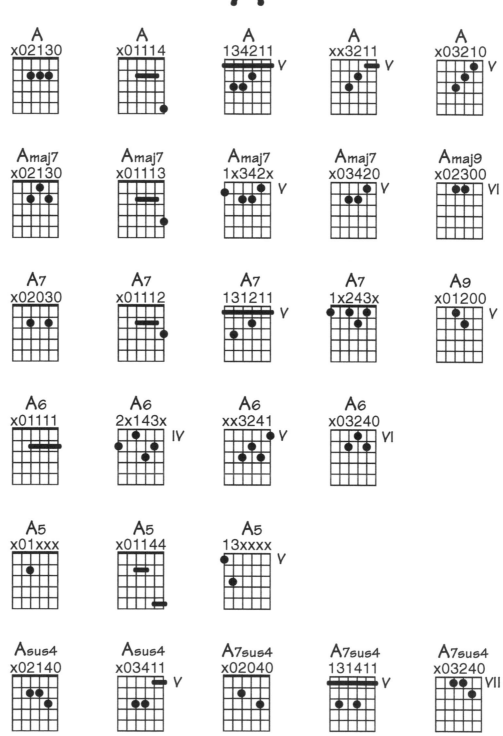

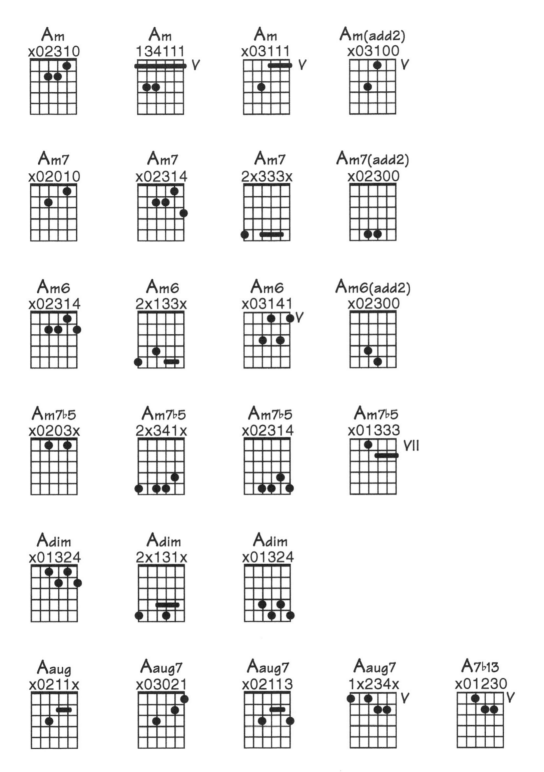

# Bb/A#

# Bb/A#*

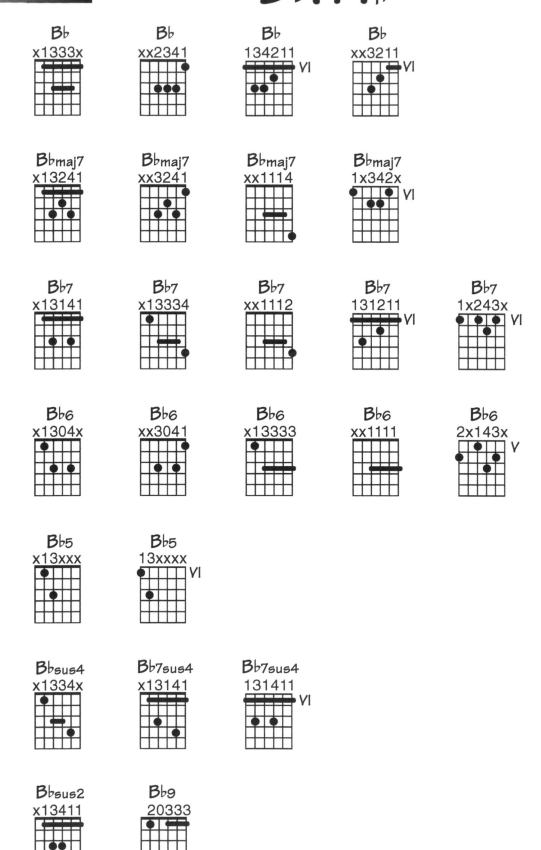

*NOTE: All chords can be written as A# or Bb.

# Bb/A#

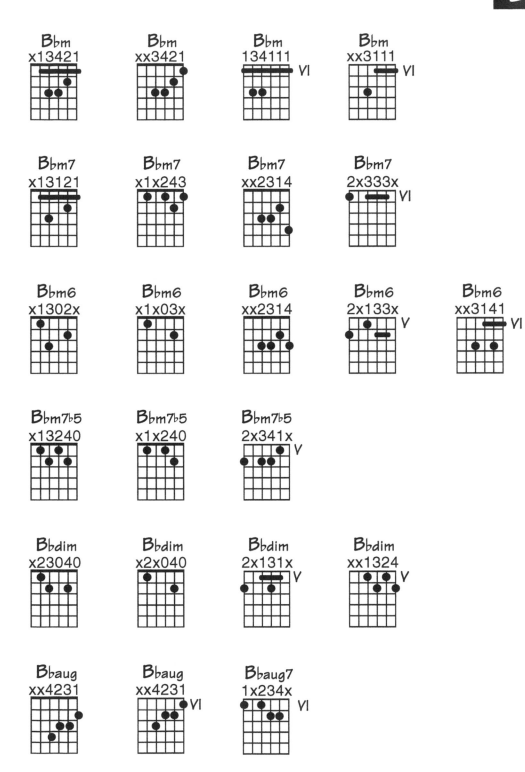

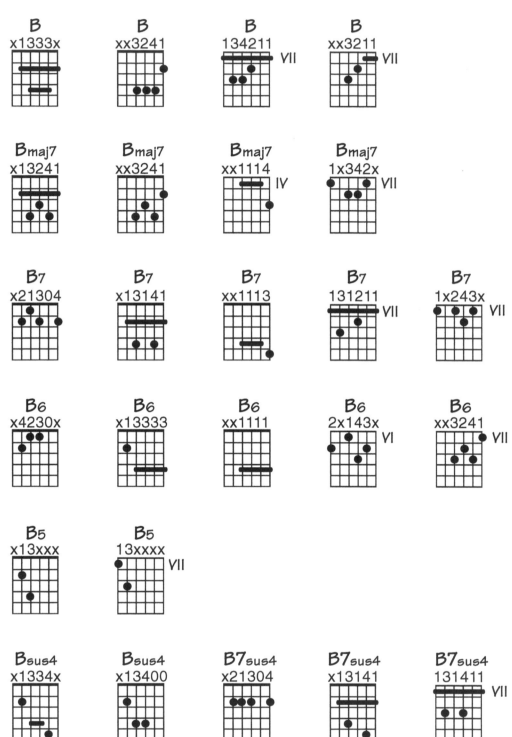

B

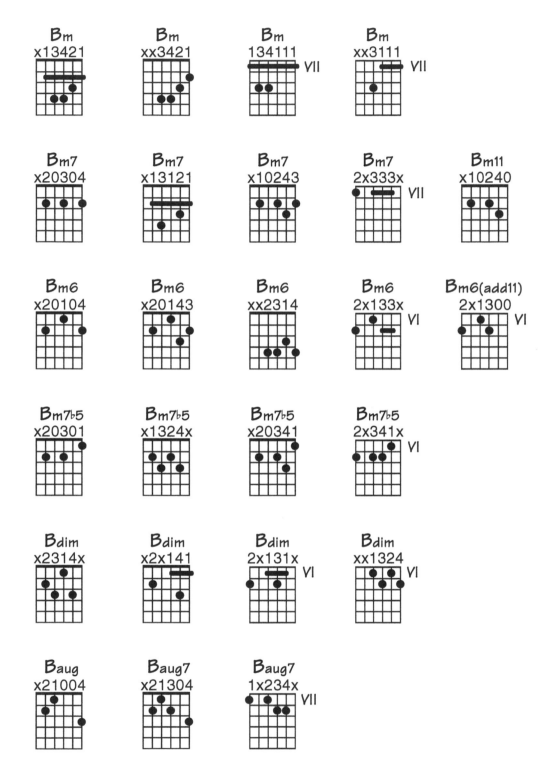

C

# C

| C | C | C | C | C | C |
|---|---|---|---|---|---|
| x32010 | x32014 | x13333x | xx2341 | 134211 VIII | xx3211 VIII |

| Cmaj7 | Cmaj7 | Cmaj7 | Cmaj7 | Cmaj7 | Cmaj7 |
|---|---|---|---|---|---|
| x32000 | x32004 | x13241 | x13400 | 1x3420 VIII | 134200 VIII |

| C7 | C7 | C7 | C7 | C7 | C7 |
|---|---|---|---|---|---|
| x32410 | x13141 | x13334 III | xx1112 V | 131211 VIII | 1x243x VIII |

| C6 | C6 | C6 | C6 | C6 |
|---|---|---|---|---|
| x42310 | x13333 | xx1111 | 2x143x VIII | xx3241 VIII |

| C5 | C5 | C5 |
|---|---|---|
| x3x014 | x13xxx | 13xxxx VIII |

| Csus4 | Csus4 | Csus4 | C7sus4 | C7sus4 |
|---|---|---|---|---|
| x3401x | xx3014 | x1334x III | x13141 III | 131411 VIII |

| Csus2 | Csus2 | Cadd2 | C9 |
|---|---|---|---|
| x30014 | x2x034 | x21034 | x21340 |

C

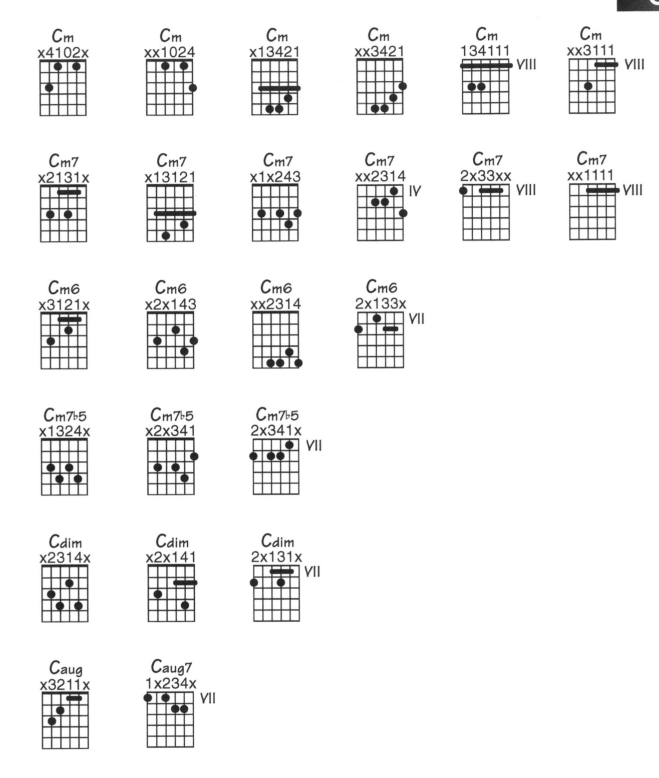

## C#/Db

# C#/Db*

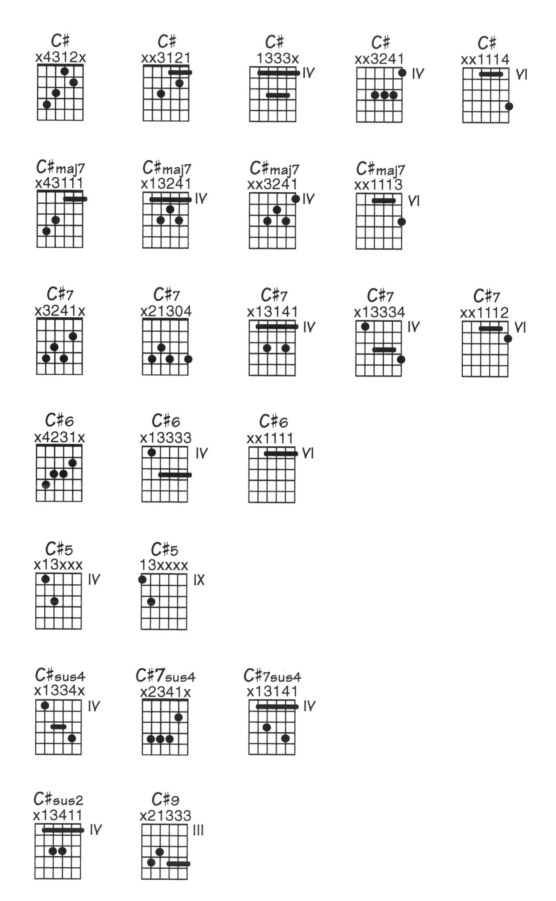

*NOTE: All chords can be written as C# or Db.

C#/Db

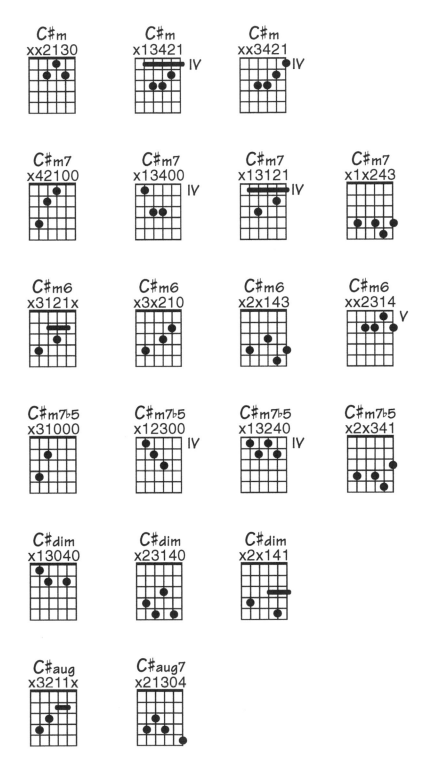

# D

## D

| D | D | D | D | D | D |
|---|---|---|---|---|---|
| xx0132 | 10023x | x1333x V | xx0341 V | xx0114 VII | xx1114 VII |

| Dmaj7 | Dmaj7 | Dmaj7 | Dmaj7 | Dmaj7 |
|---|---|---|---|---|
| xx0111 | x13241 V | xx0231 V | xx0113 | xx1114 VII |

| D7 | D7 | D7 | D7 | D7 | D7 | D7 | D7 |
|---|---|---|---|---|---|---|---|
| xx0213 | 20031x | x3241x | xx0314 | x13141 V | x13334 V | xx0112 VII | xx1112 VII |

| D6 | D6 | D6 | D6 | D6 | D6 |
|---|---|---|---|---|---|
| xx0203 | x4231x | xx0321 | x13333 V | xx0111 VII | xx1111 VII |

| D5 | D5 | D5 |
|---|---|---|
| xx01xx | xx0124 | x13xxx V |

| Dsus4 | Dsus4 | Dsus4 | D7sus4 | D7sus4 | D7sus4 |
|---|---|---|---|---|---|
| xx0134 | x1334x V | xx0341 V | xx0214 | x13141 V | xx0234 VII |

| Dsus2 | Dsus2 | Dsus2 | Dadd2 | D9 | D9 | D9 | D9 |
|---|---|---|---|---|---|---|---|
| xx0130 | x13411 V | xx0311 V | xx0230 VII | xx0210 | 200310 | x32410 | xx0310 |

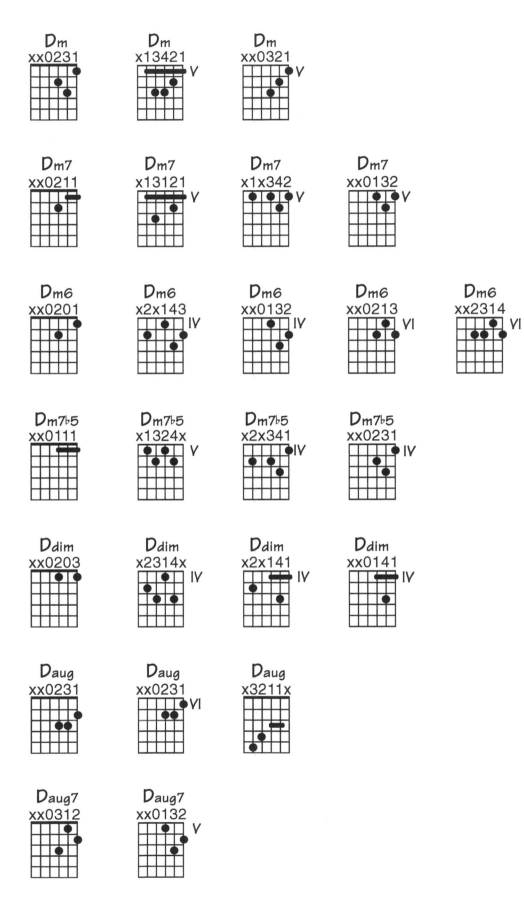

# E♭/D♯

# E♭/D♯ *

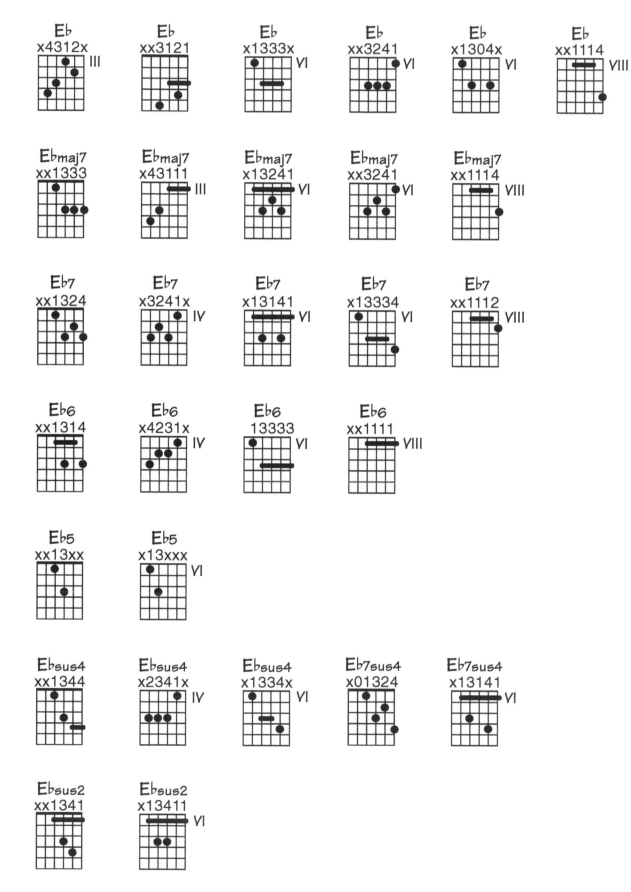

*NOTE: All chords can be written as D♯ or E♭.

## Eb/D#

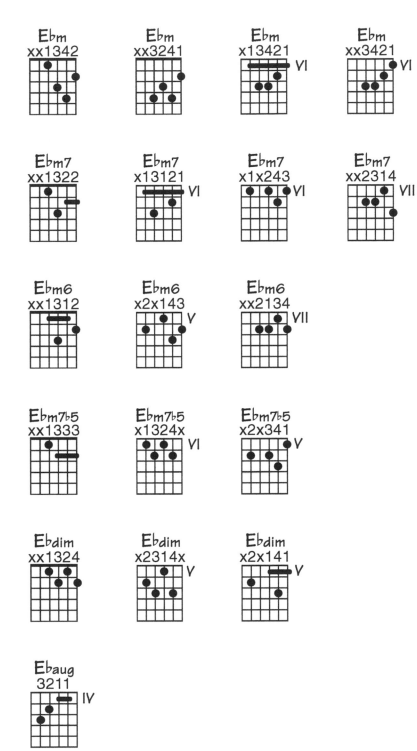

# E

## E

| E | E | E | E |
|---|---|---|---|
| 023100 | 043100 | 01333x | 0x1115 |
| | IV | VII | IX |

| Emaj7 | Emaj7 | Emaj7 | Emaj7 | Emaj7 | Emaj7 |
|---|---|---|---|---|---|
| 031200 | 0x1333 | 034100 | 043111 | 013240 | x13200 |
| | | IV | IV | VII | VII |

| E7 | E7 | E7 | E7 | E7 | E7 | E7 | E7 |
|---|---|---|---|---|---|---|---|
| 020100 | 023140 | 0x1324 | 032410 | 021300 | x13141 | x13334 | 0x1112 |
| | | | V | VI | VII | VII | IX |

| E6 | E6 | E6 | E6 | E6 | E6 | E6 |
|---|---|---|---|---|---|---|
| 023140 | 042100 | 0x1314 | 042310 | 031200 | x13333 | 0x1111 |
| | | | V | VI | VII | IX |

| E5 | E5 | E5 | E5 |
|---|---|---|---|
| 01xxxx | 012400 | x13xxx | 013400 |
| | | VII | VII |

| Esus4 | E7sus4 | E7sus4 | E7sus4 | E7sus4 |
|---|---|---|---|---|
| 023400 | 020300 | 0x1324 | x32400 | x13141 |
| | | | VII | VII |

| Esus2 | Esus2 | Eadd2 | Eadd2 | E9 | E9 |
|---|---|---|---|---|---|
| 013400 | 013411 | 023104 | 024100 | 020104 | 021333 |
| | VII | | | | VI |

E

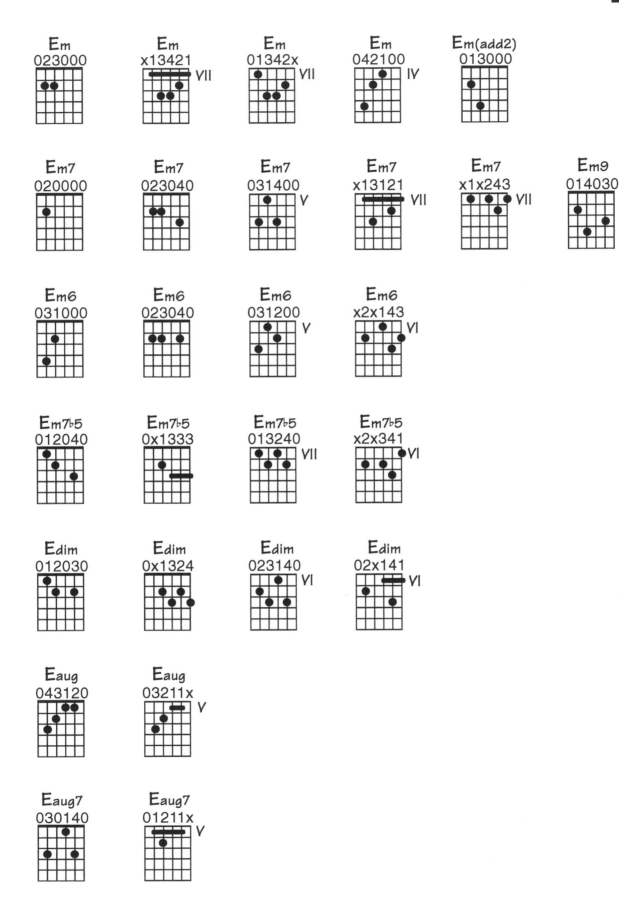

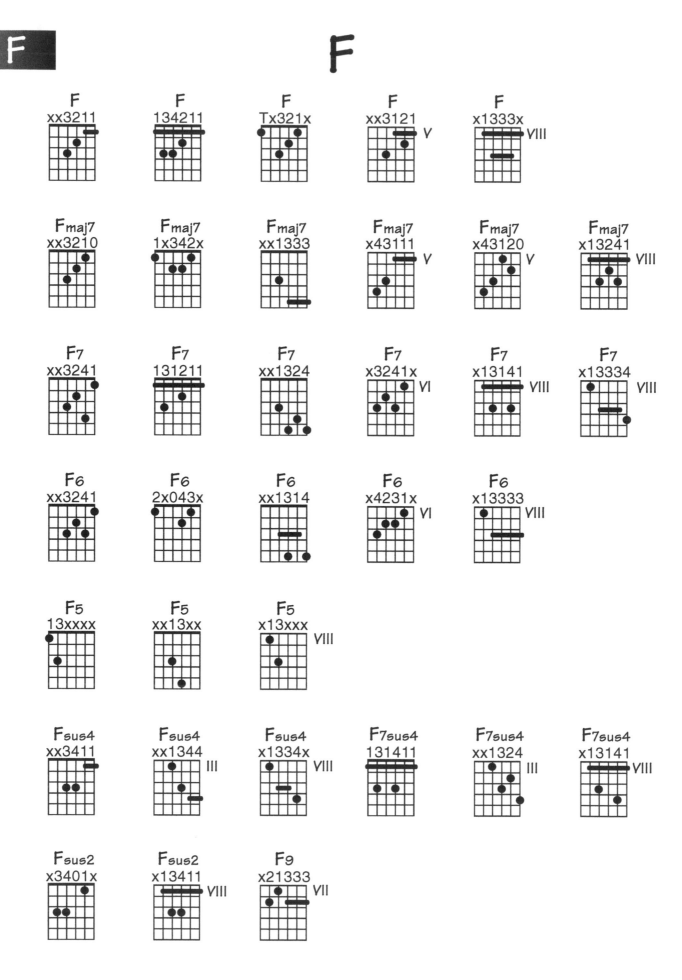

F

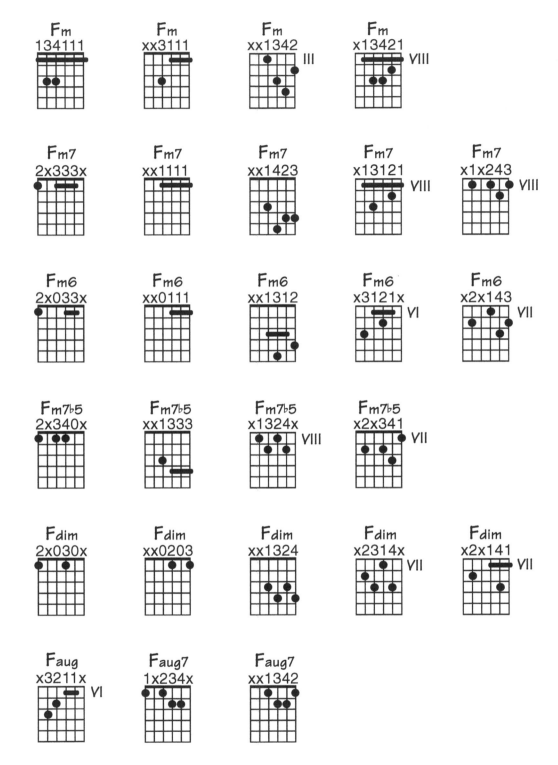

**F#/Gb**

# F#/Gb *

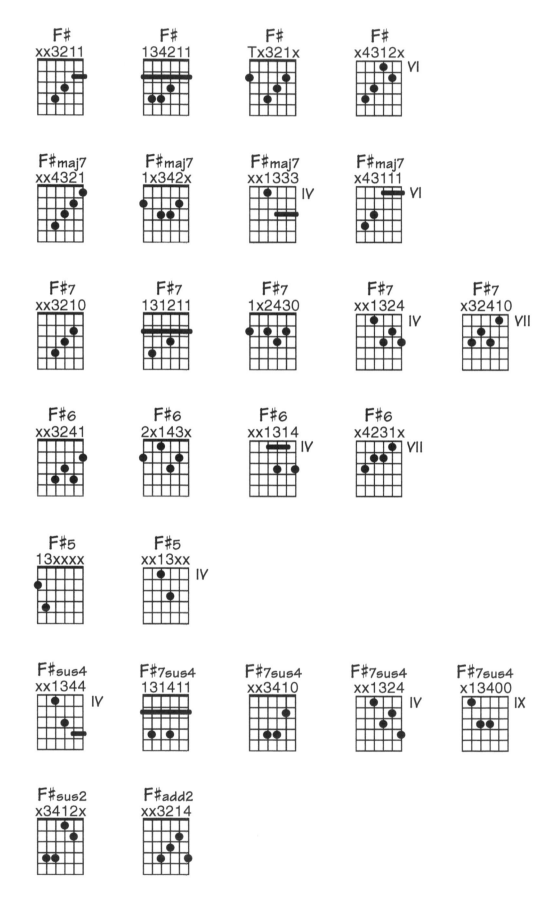

*NOTE: All chords can be written as F# or Gb.

F#/Gb

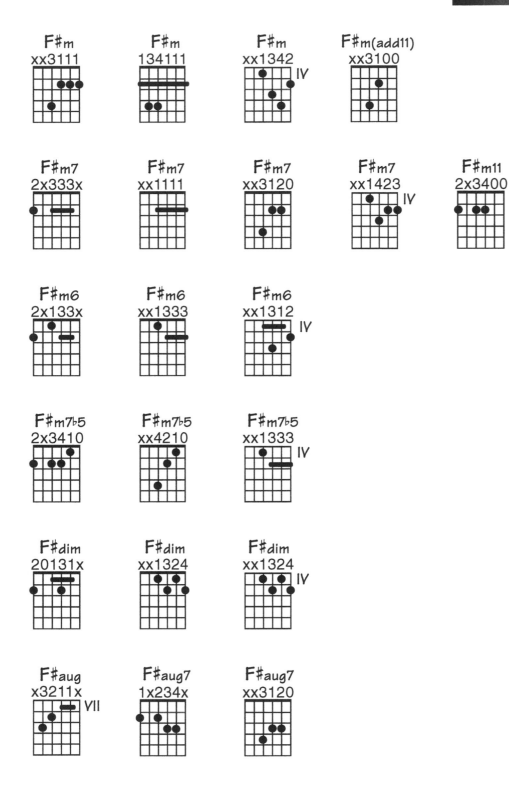

# G

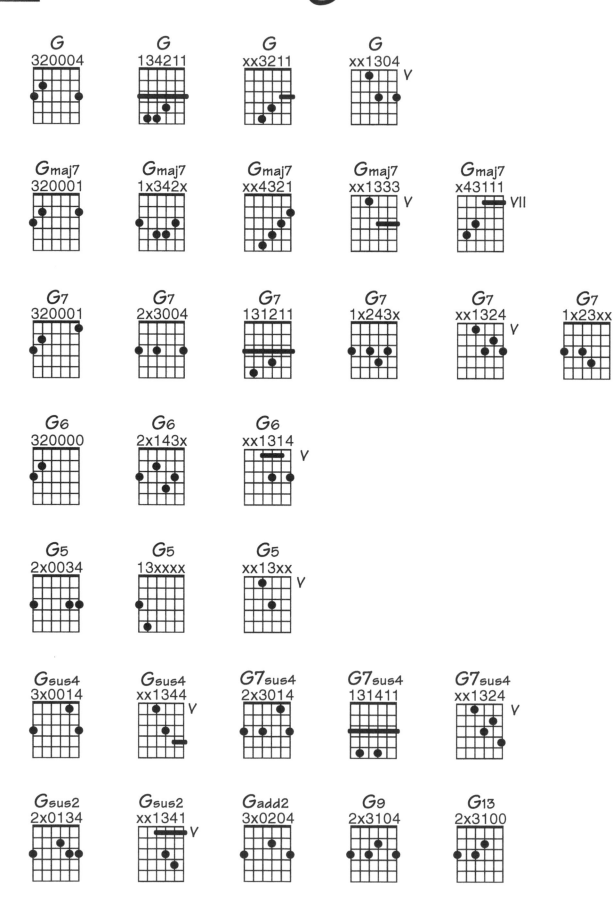

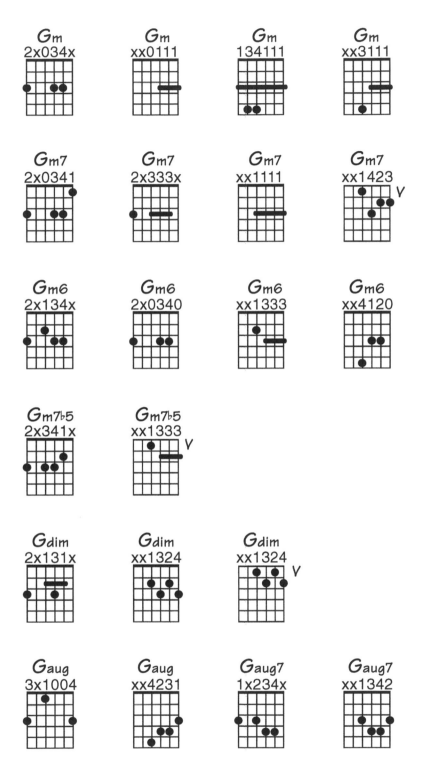

# Ab/G#

# Ab/G#*

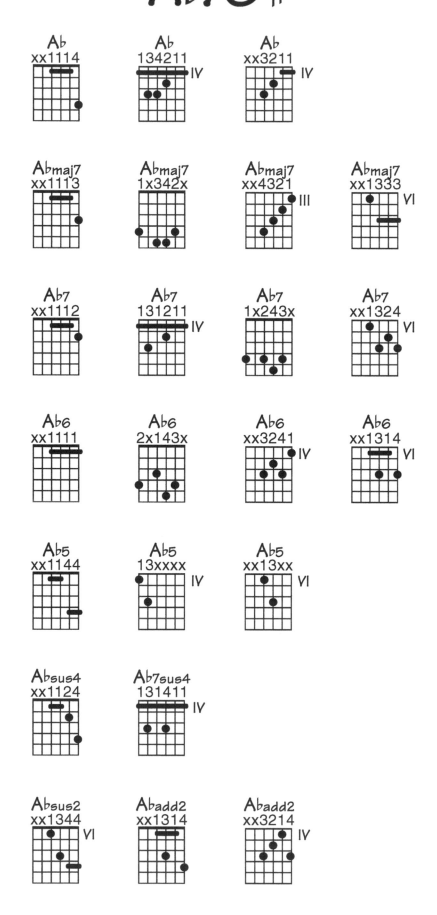

*NOTE: All chords can be written as G# or Ab.

Ab/G#

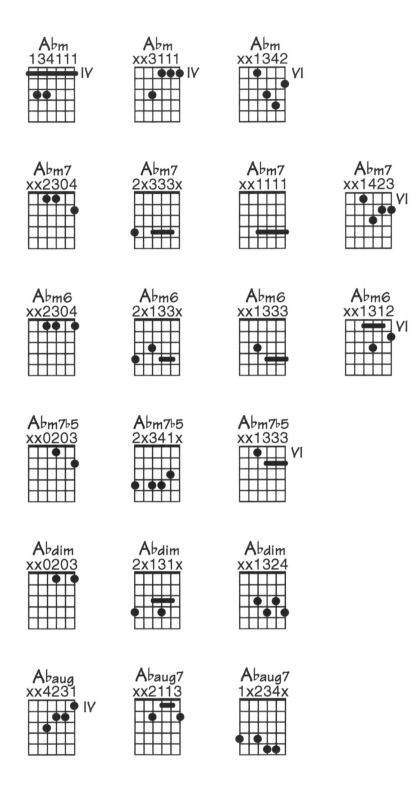

# USING A CAPO

A *capo* is designed to raise all six strings of the guitar an equal amount. For example, putting the capo on at the second fret is like tuning every string up one whole step: E becomes F♯, A becomes B, and so on, giving you F♯ B E A C♯ F♯. Now, if you've ever tuned the rest of the guitar to the low string without checking the low string itself first, you know that it doesn't matter what pitch the guitar's strings are at, as long as they're all in tune with each other. If you're in tune to yourself, your chords will be in tune—but they could be as much as a half step (or more) higher or lower than someone else's. This is a drag when you're jamming or trying to follow along by watching someone else's fingers, but if you do it on purpose, it's another story. With the capo placed at, say, the second fret, you can still form all the same chords, but those same chord shapes will now sound, in absolute terms of pitch, like a whole new set of chords. If you know just what chords they are, you can use this information constructively in a variety of ways, as we'll soon see.

## ACCOMMODATING YOUR VOICE

The most basic and important use of the capo is to change the key of a song to suit your voice. If you know a song in the key of G but find that G is kind of low for your voice, you can simply raise the pitch of the whole song by capoing. Put the capo at the second fret, and if you continue to play the same fingerings like nothing happened, the song will come out in a higher key. To know what chords you're playing, you'll have to raise the name of each chord by the same amount that you've capoed up the neck. So, if you've capoed up two frets or a whole step, your G fingering is now sounding as an A chord, your C fingering is now yielding a D, and your D fingering is sounding like an E.

If you're trying to raise the key of a tune in E for your voice, using the chords E, A, and B7, capoing to the first fret will put you in the key of F, and capoing to the second fret will put you in the relatively exotic key of F♯. Capoing three frets will put you in the key of G, which presents you with an interesting choice. You could continue to play the song using E, A, and B7, or you could remove the capo in favor of using the familiar first-position G, C, and D chords. If your voice feels just right in G♯, you could keep playing E shapes with the capo on the fourth fret, or you could use open G shapes and capo at the first fret.

Here's a chart that shows what chords you get with the five basic open chord shapes as you place the capo on frets one through seven.

| No capo | Fret 1 | 2 | 3 | 4 | 5 | 6 | 7 |
|---------|--------|---|---|---|---|---|---|
| A | A♯/B♭ | B | C | C♯/D♭ | D | D♯/E♭ | E |
| C | C♯/D♭ | D | D♯/E♭ | E | F | F♯/G♭ | G |
| D | D♯/E♭ | E | F | F♯/G♭ | G | G♯/A♭ | A |
| E | F | F♯/G♭ | G | G♯/A♭ | A | A♯/B♭ | B |
| G | G♯/A♭ | A | A♯/B♭ | B | C | C♯/D♭ | D |

## VARYING CHORD VOICINGS

As we started to see above in the E/G examples, the capo does more than just let you transpose keys. It also lets you begin to make more creative choices about what "key shapes" to use. Each of the standard major open-position keys on the guitar—G, C, E, A, and D—has distinctive qualities and possibilities. Playing uncapoed in G has a big open sound, which is widely used in country and bluegrass music. The chord voicings in the key of E often lend things a more bluesy quality, particularly because the easiest V chord to grab in the key of E is an open B7 chord, which has been used in several decades' worth of blues guitar arrangments. So if you capo at the third fret and use E chord shapes to play in the key of G, the chord shapes you've chosen are going to change the overall character of your song arrangement. You may still be playing the same chords, but you're playing different chord shapes, and that can make all the difference in the world.

For a good example of how to use this phenomenon creatively, check out Bob Dylan's recording "Don't Think Twice, It's Alright." The song is in the key of E, but Dylan capoes at the fourth fret and uses chord shapes from the family of the key of C—C, F, G7, and so on. The results are more Mississippi John Hurt than Mance Lipscomb, and suit the tone of the song well. Likewise, to create the guitar hooks for the Beatles song "Here Comes the Sun," in the key of G, George Harrison capoes at the seventh fret and then uses chord shapes from the key of D: D, G, A, etc. Playing so high up the neck lends the guitar part a shimmer it wouldn't have if it were played in open position.

## LOWERING THE KEY

You can also use a capo to lower the key. It sounds unlikely, but check it out. Suppose you had a I–IV–V song in G (i.e., it uses the chords G, C, and D). Maybe G is too high a key for your voice, and you think, "Man, if this song was in F it would be perfect. I need the anti-capo." Well, short of detuning your guitar a whole step, the anti-capo remains a mere dream of poets and madmen alike, but there is an alternative. Try capoing at the third fret and using chord shapes from the key of D. The capo will make your D sound like an F, your G sound like a B♭, and your A sound like a C. That gives you F, B♭, and C, which are the I, IV, and V in the key of F.

B♭ is another key that's hard to play in. If you've learned a song in C that's too high for you, you can rework it using G shapes and a capo on the third fret. At that capo position, G becomes B♭, C becomes E♭, and D becomes an F—giving you B♭, E♭, and F, or the I, IV, and V in the key of B♭.

## BYPASSING OTHER HARD-TO-PLAY CHORDS

As you go through songbooks, learning new songs, you may come across tunes that look a lot harder than you thought they would. Either they're in a difficult key, like E♭ or D♭, or they have one or more minor or dominant seventh chords that don't have any obvious open-position fingering. In some cases the song may have been recorded using a capo, or it may simply have been written without the guitar in mind, as in the case of most jazz compositions and Tin Pan Alley standards. Either way, the capo can occasionally help you out of a bind like this, or at least give you some creative choices.

In the case of songs in flat keys, the capo can generally put the song into one of the five guitar-friendly keys. For example, a song in the key of E♭ has the I, IV, and V chords E♭, A♭, and B♭, none of which lie well in open position on the guitar. But if you capo to the first fret and play the chord shapes D, G, and A, they'll come out sounding as E♭, A♭, and B♭.

Frequently when you make this sort of adjustment, some of the more awkward-looking minor chords evaporate as well. If you have a song in A♭, the I, IV, and V will be A♭, D♭, and E♭, and the ii, iii, and vi chords will be B♭m, Cm, and Fm, all of which require barre chords. Capo to the first fret, however, and use chords from the key of G, and peace is restored to your troubled fingers: the shapes for G, C, and D will give you your I, IV, and V, and the shapes for Am, Bm, and Em will give you your ii, iii, and vi chords.

Is it cheating? That's for you to decide. If that's how the recording was created in the first place, then by using the capo you're just getting more accurately at what the songwriter or interpreter of that song had in mind. You're solving a puzzle, trying to figure out what's happening on the guitar without the benefit of any visual clues. If a song was composed in a flat key initially, like a Broadway standard, it was in all likelihood created without any particular concern for whether it would be easy or hard to play on the guitar. In that case, as you try to figure out a way to adapt the song to your instrument, it's really more a matter of taste and idiom whether you use a capo to enable you to play open chords or figure out how to play the song using movable chord shapes like barre chords.

## LEARNING OFF OF RECORDS

As you try to learn songs off of recordings, keep in mind that your favorite guitarist may have used a capo in the studio. As you check out a song, guitar in hand, listen for the sound of open strings, which means the guitarist is using open chords rather than barre chords. If you hear that open-string jangle, try to identify which chord shapes you're hearing based on your own familiarity with the sound of the five basic shapes—G, C, D, A, and E. If you hear what sounds like a C chord shape, but your own C chord doesn't match up when you play along, try gradually capoing your way up the neck until the sounds do match.

Alternatively, you can try to determine what sounds like the predominant chord in the song, and find the root note of that chord on your guitar on the sixth or fifth string. If you find that the root note is, say, the fourth fret on the fifth string, or C♯, you can try a few different capo positions to see what sounds most like the recording. Two good guesses in this particular case would be: capo at the first fret and play a C shape (C up a half step is C♯), or capo at the fourth fret and play an A shape (A up four frets, or two whole steps, is also C♯).

Once you've found a single chord on your guitar that matches the recording, you can experiment with the other chords that are usually used with it (see Chords in a Key). See if you can find any more shapes that match with other chords you hear in the song. Keep in mind that the first chord you've found may not be the I chord of the song. In other words, if the first chord you pin down is a C, that could be the I chord for the key of C, suggesting the presence of chords like F and G, or it could be, say, the IV chord in the key of G, suggesting that you try out chords like G and D next. It could even be the V chord in the key of F, suggesting choices like F and B♭.

If the song is played entirely with barre chords, you won't need the capo at all, because you can just play the various movable chord forms wherever they match up with what's on the recording.

# CHORDS IN A KEY

We've talked a bit about how to use the capo to start figuring out songs off of records and how to move around the key of a song for your voice. But how do you know what chords are likely to be in a song in the first place?

You can use the major scale to get a handle on what chords generally appear in a key. The chords in a key come from building triad shapes from the notes available in that key's major scale. Let's take the key of G major. The notes of the G-major scale are G, A, B, C, D, E, F♯, and G. If we go ahead and build a triad beginning with the note G and using only the notes available to us in the scale, the result is G, B, D—a G-major triad. Since this chord is built on the first degree, or note, of the scale, it is referred to as the I chord ("the one chord"). Moving on, if we build a triad off of the second degree of the scale, A, again using only the notes available to us in the G-major scale itself, the result is A, C, E—an A-minor triad. Since this chord is built off of the second degree of the scale, it is referred to as the ii chord. (The lowercase Roman numeral indicates that this is a minor chord, while the capital Roman numeral I indicates that the G chord is major.)

Following this process through for the remaining five notes, we arrive at the following collection of chords:

| G | Am | Bm | C | D | Em | F♯dim |
|---|----|----|---|---|----|-------|
| I | ii | iii | IV | V | vi | vii dim |

Since the intervals of the major scale remain consistent no matter what the key, it is also true that the sequence of chords derived this way will remain consistent from key to key, leading us to the generalization that in every major key, the I, IV, and V chords will be major and the ii, iii, and vi chords will be minor. Which further means that in the five basic open keys of the guitar, E, A, D, G, and C, we can count on the following chords being the most likely to surface in each of those keys.

| Key | I | ii | iii | IV | V | vi | vii dim |
|-----|---|-----|-----|----|---|-----|---------|
| E | E | F♯m | G♯m | A | B | C♯m | D♯dim |
| A | A | Bm | C♯m | D | E | F♯m | G♯dim |
| D | D | Em | F♯m | G | A | Bm | C♯dim |
| G | G | Am | Bm | C | D | Em | F♯dim |
| C | C | Dm | Em | F | G | Am | Bdim |

All very well and good, and this will help you as you hunt around for that missing chord you can't figure out on the recording. But what about the song that seems impossible to play in the first place, because it isn't in one of these keys?

Let's take a hypothetical situation: You flip open a songbook and there on the page is a song you're dying to play, only it opens with G minor. G minor! Who wants to play that? Followed by the equally doomsome B♭ and the not-so-fun-to-play F! Meanwhile, there's a perfectly innocent C running around in there too. What's going on? You've heard this song played a billion times, it just sounds like simple strumming on the CD, with big open chords . . .

Well, now, hang on. We've got three major chords here, B♭, C and F. Juggle them around a little and you might see that the song's in the key of F, with F, B♭, and C serving as I, IV, and V, and Gm as the ii chord.

With a little creative capoing, you can make all those not-especially-open chords vaporize in a flash. Put your capo at the third fret. Now, an open Em chord will create the sound of a Gm chord. One down! Next, a G shape will give you the sound of B♭. An A-chord shape gives you a different-sounding but equally open C-chord sound, and a D shape yields the sound of an F chord. What you've done is taken the chord shapes and harmonic relationships of the key of D and transposed them up three frets so that they sound in the key of F. No muss, no fuss, no awkward fingerings—just big, ringy open chords as far as the ear can hear. You can use the table below to troubleshoot seemingly difficult keys, finding a combination of open chord shapes and capo position to re-create the sound of the key you need using familiar and easy-to-play voicings.

## KEY-OF-E FINGERINGS

| Capo | I | ii | iii | IV | V | vi | viidim |
|---|---|---|---|---|---|---|---|
| None | E | F#m | G#m | A | B | C#m | D#dim |
| 1st fr. | F | Gm | Am | B♭ | C | Dm | Edim |
| 2nd | G♭ | A♭m | B♭m | C♭ | D♭ | E♭m | Fdim |
| 3rd | G | Am | Bm | C | D | Em | F#dim |
| 4th | A♭ | B♭m | Cm | D♭ | E♭ | Fm | Gdim |
| 5th | A | Bm | C#m | D | E | F#m | G#dim |
| 6th | B♭ | Cm | Dm | E♭ | F | Gm | Adim |
| 7th | B | C#m | D#m | E | F# | G#m | A#dim |

## KEY-OF-A FINGERINGS

| Capo | I | ii | iii | IV | V | vi | viidim |
|---|---|---|---|---|---|---|---|
| None | A | Bm | C#m | D | E | F#m | G#dim |
| 1st | B♭ | Cm | Dm | E♭ | F | Gm | Adim |
| 2nd | B | C#m | D#m | E | F# | G#m | A#dim |
| 3rd | C | Dm | Em | F | G | Am | Bdim |
| 4th | D♭ | E♭m | Fm | G♭ | A♭ | B♭m | Cdim |
| 5th | D | Em | F#m | G | A | Bm | C#dim |
| 6th | E♭ | Fm | Gm | A♭ | B♭ | Cm | Ddim |
| 7th | E | F#m | G#m | A | B | C#m | D#dim |

## KEY-OF-D FINGERINGS

| Capo | I | ii | iii | IV | V | vi | viidim |
|---|---|---|---|---|---|---|---|
| None | D | Em | F#m | G | A | Bm | C#dim |
| 1st | E♭ | Fm | Gm | A♭ | B♭ | Cm | Ddim |
| 2nd | E | F#m | G#m | A | B | C#m | D#dim |
| 3rd | F | Gm | Am | B♭ | C | Dm | Edim |
| 4th | G♭ | A♭m | B♭m | C♭ | D♭ | E♭m | Fdim |
| 5th | G | Am | Bm | C | D | Em | F#dim |
| 6th | A♭ | B♭m | Cm | D♭ | E♭ | Fm | Gdim |
| 7th | A | Bm | C#m | D | E | F#m | G#dim |

## KEY-OF-G FINGERINGS

| Capo | I | ii | iii | IV | V | vi | viidim |
|---|---|---|---|---|---|---|---|
| None | G | Am | Bm | C | D | Em | F#dim |
| 1st | A♭ | B♭m | Cm | D♭ | E♭ | Fm | Gdim |
| 2nd | A | Bm | C#m | D | E | F#m | G#dim |
| 3rd | B♭ | Cm | Dm | E♭ | F | Gm | Adim |
| 4th | B | C#m | D#m | E | F# | G#m | A#dim |
| 5th | C | Dm | Em | F | G | Am | Bdim |
| 6th | D♭ | E♭m | Fm | G♭ | A♭ | B♭m | Cdim |
| 7th | D | Em | F#m | G | A | Bm | C#dim |

## KEY-OF-C FINGERINGS

| Capo | I | ii | iii | IV | V | vi | viidim |
|---|---|---|---|---|---|---|---|
| None | C | Dm | Em | F | G | Am | Bdim |
| 1st | D♭ | E♭m | Fm | G♭ | A♭ | B♭m | Cdim |
| 2nd | D | Em | F#m | G | A | Bm | C#dim |
| 3rd | E♭ | Fm | Gm | A♭ | B♭ | Cm | Ddim |
| 4th | E | F#m | G#m | A | B | C#m | D#dim |
| 5th | F | Gm | Am | B♭ | C | Dm | Edim |
| 6th | G♭ | A♭m | B♭m | C♭ | D♭ | E♭m | Fdim |
| 7th | G | Am | Bm | C | D | Em | F#dim |

## OTHER LIKELY SUSPECTS

There are other chords that often infiltrate the diatonic world of the seven chords that officially belong in each key. Let's look at a few of these and categorize them so that you can recognize them when they appear and perhaps use them in your own songwriting.

One of the most common nondiatonic chords to show up, particularly in ragtime and swing tunes, is something called a *secondary dominant* chord. The only dominant chord that really belongs in any key is the V chord. But you can also have a dominant chord a fifth up from any of the diatonic chords in the key, if it's leading into that diatonic chord. For example, in the key of G, the V chord is D. It's common, however, to see the chord progression at right.

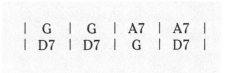

A7 is the V chord in the key of D, so when you hear the A7 in this chord progression, it leads your ear to the D7. In this situation A7 is also referred to as a *borrowed* chord, because while playing in the key of G, we're borrowing the A7 from the key of D.

Another likely place for a secondary dominant is leading into one of the three minor chords: the ii, the iii, or the vi. In the key of G, that would mean playing E7 to Am, F♯7 to Bm, or B7 to Em. At right is a progression in the key of G that includes B7 and E7 in this way.

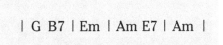

Blues chord progressions often deviate from the standard diatonic harmony by using dominant seventh chords for the I and the IV as well as the V. This doesn't necessarily square with the diatonic idea of building up each chord from the notes available in the major scale of a given key, but it's the logical result of the music's origins in African as well as European sensibilities. The basic 12-bar blues chord progression often includes just dominant I, IV, and V chords; here's one common version of a form that has many subtle variations, shown first in the abstract and then in the key of E.

The ♭III and ♭VII chords are major chords built off of the flat third and flat seventh degrees of the scale. Since the major scale has neither a ♭3 nor a ♭7, the ♭III and ♭VII chords are not diatonic to any major key. These two sounds have their origins in the minor pentatonic melodies of the blues and the modal melodies of the British Isles, and are often used in more contemporary music as well. Let's see how they work in the key of A. The ♭3 in the key of A is C and the ♭7 is G, so the ♭III chord in the key of A is C major and the ♭VII chord is G. So you could, for example, have a chord progression in A that included G (the ♭VII) along with A, D, and E (the I, IV, and V).

To sum up, here are all of the possibilities we've discussed for the chords available in one key.

*Diatonic*

| I | ii | iii | IV | V | vi | vii dim |

*Nondiatonic*
Secondary dominant:

II7 (as V7 of V)     III7 (as V7 of vi)     VI7 (as V7 of ii)     VII7 (as V7 of iii)

Blues:

I7     IV7

Modal:

♭III     ♭VII

# ABOUT THE AUTHOR

David Hamburger is a performer and writer who lives in Austin, Texas. He has been playing folk and blues music since first picking up a guitar at the age of 12 and has been on the faculty of the National Guitar Workshop since 1988. Hamburger's guitar, slide guitar, and Dobro playing can be heard on his solo albums *King of the Brooklyn Delta* (Chester, 1994) and *Indigo Rose* (Chester, 1999) as well as on numerous independent recordings.

Hamburger is the author of several other books, including *The Complete Acoustic Guitar Method* and *Acoustic Guitar Slide Basics*, and has contributed dozens of lessons and articles to *Guitar Player* and *Acoustic Guitar* magazines. For a discography, performance schedule, and other information, visit his Web site at www.davidhamburger.com.

## ACKNOWLEDGMENTS

Thanks to Jeffrey Pepper Rodgers for his invaluable assistance in wrestling this book's purpose to the ground, to David Lusterman for conceiving the *Acoustic Guitar Method* series in the first place, and to the editorial staff of *Acoustic Guitar*. Special thanks to Susan Hamburger, for playing me *Sgt. Pepper* at exactly the right moment; to Peter Wallach ("*the* Peter Wallach—the man who never calls back?"); to Jim Blau, for showing up with all those lists of questions; and most of all to Catherine Berry, who remains convinced that I am, in fact, a rock star.

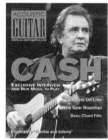

# ABOUT STRING LETTER PUBLISHING

*Sring Letter Publishing*, which was founded in 1986, is the source for acoustic music magazines and books. We serve musicians, aficionados, and listeners with news, information, advice, and entertainment through a wide selection of products. Our specialty is music where songs and stringed instruments play a major role: roots, jazz, blues, rock, classical, and other traditional and contemporary styles. From songbooks to guidebooks to pictorial reference works, String Letter books are enduring resources for acoustic musicians and students who want to improve their playing skills, expand their musical horizons, and become more knowledgeable about instruments and gear. Learn more at www.stringletter.com.

String Letter publishes *Acoustic Guitar,* the magazine for all acoustic guitar players, from beginners to performing professionals. Through interviews, reviews, workshops, sheet music, and song transcriptions, *Acoustic Guitar* readers learn music from around the globe and get to know the artists who create it. With product reviews and expert advice, *Acoustic Guitar* also helps readers become smarter buyers and owners of acoustic guitars and guitar gear. For more informtion, visit us on the Web at www.acousticguitar.com.